Brothers *in Murder*

Jo Ann Wiblin

ISBN 978-1-63874-405-4 (paperback)
ISBN 978-1-63874-406-1 (digital)

Christian Faith Publishing
832 Park Avenue
Meadville, PA 16335
www.christianfaithpublishing.com

Printed in the United States of America

Contents

Illustrations

Map of Murder Sites

Forker's Cafe

McCann

Jones

WigWam

Martin

Scouted Houses

Annick

Gary's Home

Introduction

Any man's death diminishes me,
Because I am involved in mankind.
            —John Donne (1573–1631)

SINCE THE TIME OF Cain and Abel, murder has been the most feared and yet the most fascinating crime of mankind. Once done, it cannot be undone, whether by a repentant killer, by the victim's grieving family, or by a court system bent on rehabilitation or revenge. Its very finality allows no effective alternative—money can be replaced, but a life is irreplaceable.

Over the centuries, society has drastically altered its views on murder and murderers. Primitive societies did not regard a murderer as dangerous as we do today. Probably in those prehistoric times, there were few murders with malice aforethought as we think of that crime. More often, the crimes were probably manslaughter as in self-defense, accident, or the heat of passion (Biggs, 8–9).

In those days, the custom was to regard murder as a crime to property. Thus, the family or tribe to which a murdered victim belonged was entitled to retribution by killing either the murderer or some other member of his family equal in importance to the original victim (Brophy, 12). This sometimes led to a domino effect, which resulted in family feuds similar to the infamous Hatfields and McCoys' long-standing battle. Small societies could not long afford such large-scale destruction, so a new system evolved. A monetary value was placed on the victim according to his status in the community, and the offender was required to pay this fine. Thus, a great deal was paid for a chieftain, very little for an elderly slave or young female child (Brophy, 12). Eventually, even this punishment fell into disfavor as some families collected the fine and still partook of revenge. It finally became imperative that the power to punish be vested in a disinterested party in the form of a leader or other representative of the community. Thus the forerunner of our modern-day judicial system was born.

Homicide, as we know it today, refers to "the killing of another person" and may either be criminal or noncriminal. The criminal type, or murder, may be voluntary or nonvoluntary. Voluntary homicide, or first-degree homicide, must usually contain an element of intent by the offender—that is, he must intend to cause serious bodily harm to his victim. Involuntary homicide, or manslaughter, is also a criminal offense but is usually the result of the offender's negligence rather than his intention to cause harm (Wolfgang, 16). An example of manslaughter would be a driver's poorly maintained brakes, causing the death of another. It is the driver's negligence to properly maintain his brakes that makes him liable. However, because he did not intend to cause the other person's death, he is not guilty of murder. According to the law, an adult murderer must consciously and sanely intend the death of the victim to be found guilty of murder (Brophy, 13). The only exceptions to this rule are two—murders done in self-defense or homicide performed as a legal duty by a peace officer or executioner (Wolfgang, 16).

The primary subject of this paper will be to analyze a series of murders that occurred in the central Ohio area beginning in late 1977 and ending almost exactly one year later, in December 1978. During that time, ten people lost their lives to a killer or killers unknown. The crimes were distributed in three counties but always near an interstate highway access road, suggesting that the offender used this route as an escape. Later, arrested and convicted were two brothers, Thaddeus Charles Lewingdon and Gary James Lewingdon. Like the Mississippi River in Mark Twain's novel of Huckleberry Finn, the miles of concrete highway act as an artery and are a constant theme throughout the tale—but unlike Twain's story, ours is one of evil and bloodshed.

Murders that are not simultaneous are called serial murders rather than mass murders. Some murders are multiple and simultaneous, while others are multiple but carried out over an extended period of time. It is these serial murders which, by their very nature, hold a special horror for the townspeople where they occur. Where will the killer strike next? What is his pattern? People begin to suspect their friends and neighbors and to fear for their very lives. An entire community is held hostage to the criminal's mind for as long as he remains free.

These particular crimes were dubbed by a local newspaper as the .22 caliber killings since all the murders were from a weapon of that type. The victims were shot many times in an overkill method, and almost all were shot at close range in the head. The motive appeared to be robbery, and in fact, the final capture was a result of the murderer's using a credit card of one of his victims—he was Christmas shopping.

The succeeding sections of this paper are a synopsis of the crimes themselves. Because of the interruption to the story, I have chosen not to insert footnotes or other references. However, almost all the material was taken directly from the Charles Lewingdon's trial transcripts, which included a verbatim transcription of his taped confessions. Minor details were taken from a newspaper interview that Delaine Lewingdon gave to the *Columbus Citizen-Journal* dated January 27, 1979. I have attempted to blend the myriad of disjointed details into a digestible narrative whole, with a minimum of dramatic additions.

Prologue

GARY LEWINGDON NEEDED MONEY. He never seemed to have enough to pay his bills, especially since he had met Delaine. She and her three children were expensive to support. A bachelor of long standing, Gary had taken the plunge and begun living with Delaine Grumman in Newark, Ohio.

Because of the financial problems, he had been trying to persuade his brother, Charles, to help him with a break-in at a store he knew. Charles, with a wife and children of his own, was on welfare and needed money worse than Gary. Charles and his family had moved to Chicago where he soon hurt his back and had to return to the central Ohio area. Consequently, he was out of work, while Gary had worked steadily at Rockwell Manufacturing in Columbus for ten years. Relentlessly, Gary kept up the pressure for assistance, until finally, Charles gave in. That weekend, he didn't feel well—in fact, he had a temperature of 102 degrees, but he wanted to help his brother. He hoped this would satisfy him. Besides, he was in need of some money himself.

On the night of September 23–24, 1977, a break-in occurred at the Western Auto Store at 3510 Cleveland Avenue in Columbus, Ohio. The brothers pried open the door with tools taken from a leather satchel, and once inside, they broke the glass of the gun display case. They stole at least eight guns that night—a .25 caliber automatic, a .38 caliber revolver, a .22 caliber Stoeger Luger semi-automatic, two rifles, some shotguns, and one or two other rifles. They also stole some color TV sets and one stereo.

Charles kept the Stoeger Luger and two other guns. He hoped Gary would be satisfied, but Gary began planning a murder/robbery near his home. He cased the place and learned the routine in the little bar. Soon, Charles would use the Stoeger Luger in the cold-blooded murder of nine people.

Forker's Cafe

Joyce Vermillion, Karen Dodrill

DECEMBER 10, 1977, WAS a bitterly cold winter day in Newark, Ohio. Christmas was just around the corner, and shopping was in everyone's minds. Some, however, were entertaining themselves in a shabby bar known as Forker's Cafe near the railroad tracks. On either side of the bar were pawnshops and disintegrating houses. Just behind the building was a vast, grassy area that had been cleared by the Ohio Department of Highways in preparation for a new freeway access from the south and west end of town. As these projects go, however, funds ran out before the project could be completed. Thus, one entire block of homes had been leveled of buildings—leaving trees, shrubs, and grass in a parklike atmosphere.

The street thus left with an open view to the rear of these businesses was Pine Street—a crowded row of homes and apartments. Most were in need of paint, and many front yards were strewn with children's toys and discarded car parts. Some two blocks north was the home of Gary Lewingdon and Delaine Grumman.

Joyce Vermillion, thirty-seven, was at work that evening in Forker's Cafe. She was night manager, so it was her duty to close for the night. As soon as the last customer left, she busily counted the night's receipts and placed them in the safe, shut off all the appliances, and cleaned the counters. Her friend, Karen Dodrill, thirty-three, waited patiently to take her home. Finally, Joyce picked up her purse and a paper bag with the sandwich she had made for her husband and made ready to leave. She had difficulty locking the security bar across the back door, and it took them some fifteen minutes to secure it. Finally, they exited from the front door on to Union Street.

Stinging cold struck their faces as they went outside. The temperature was fifteen below, and a brisk wind produced a chill factor of forty-five degrees below zero. The women pulled their scarves closer around their faces as they turned the corner toward Pine Street to where Karen's car was parked. As Karen fumbled for her car keys, two men in ski masks stepped out from behind the garage across the small side street. Frightened, Karen and Joyce dropped their purses and backed up the one step to the concrete porch of the back door of the bar.

One man spoke quickly. "Where's the money?" he asked.

"It's inside the safe," Joyce replied.

"Let's go get it," the man ordered.

"It took us fifteen minutes to get the door locked, and we can't hardly get back in."

Joyce watched the other man as he steadily held a gun with a long round attachment protruding from the front end pointing at her head. She hoped they would accept her explanation.

He spoke again, but this time to the man with the gun.

"Do it," Gary said to Charles.

The women froze.

"Are you sure?"

"Yes, do it."

Charles opened fire. Muffled shots struck the women as they fell against the building.

Bullets slammed into Joyce with ferocious accuracy—one penetrated the forehead; one grazed her left cheek and earlobe, bruising her neck and shoulders; one hit her left side, two to three inches below her armpit; one struck seven and a half inches below her left armpit; and one entered her left shoulder and exited at the middle of her chest—a total of five shots in all.

The same gun delivered seven wounds to Karen Dodrill, the patron of the bar who was doing her friend a favor by taking her home on a cold night. She was hit on the right side of the face by four bullets and on the left side of the torso by three. One bullet to the right temporal region of her head exited just in front of her right ear.

The women crashed, dying instantly, onto the rear porch of the bar, while the possessions clutched in their hands fell to the ground by the porch. Karen Dodrill's keys fell a few feet from the bodies, as did Joyce Vermillion's sandwich. The two men grabbed the women's purses and ran the half block toward Pine Street to where Charles's 1967 Ford station wagon was parked.

As daylight arrived, Robert Derringer waited at the stoplight in front of Forker's Cafe. His car struggled to clear the window of frost as he turned the corner onto Wilson Street. Slowing for a patch of ice there, he glanced to his right absently. As he passed the rear of the bar, he noticed a woman lying on the porch. Fearing that she had fallen on the slippery walk and had crawled up on the porch to warm herself, he stopped the car and went over to her. As he moved closer, he recognized her as Joyce Vermillion. Then he saw the other woman. Suddenly, he knew something was seriously wrong. There were "all those shells laying around, those .22 caliber shells." He tried to run across the street to the garage there for help but fell on the ice. He shouted to the owner to have his secretary call the emergency squad and the police.

Meanwhile, Larry Vermillion, Joyce's husband, had become worried about his wife. Usually, she was home by 3:00 or 3:30 a.m., but it was already 8:00 a.m., and she had not yet come. He dressed the baby and headed for the sitter's house. As he passed Forker's, he saw a car in the rear and thought that maybe the bar was open. He would ask if they knew where Joyce was.

Bob Derringer, still shaken from his discovery, saw Larry coming, whom he also knew. He didn't want Larry to find his wife there. He told him not to go to the back, but Larry wouldn't listen.

The Newark paramedics, expecting to find two women suffering from exposure to the cold, arrived to find two frozen bodies riddled with bullets.

Two-and-a-half short blocks away, Delaine Grumman lay dozing on her couch. Suddenly, the door opened with a blast of cold air, and two men carrying guns entered. Gary sank into a chair as he pulled off the ski mask. Charles angrily slammed the purses down, accusing Gary of not doing his part in the murder, while

Gary, Delaine's live-in lover, protested that his gun was too noisy to use. Charles's Stoeger Luger was much quieter with the homemade silencer attached. Disappointingly, the purses contained only thirty-eight dollars and a small amount of drugs. Charles kept all the money since he was on welfare. Gary pocketed a pair of nail clippers he found in one purse. Charles said he would throw the purses in a dumpster and that next time would be better.

McCann

Robert "Mickey" McCann, Dorothy Marie McCann, Christine Herdman

ROBERT "MICKEY" MCCANN, OWNER of the El Dorado Club on Sullivant Avenue on the west side of Columbus, was well-known to the police. His club had been cited numerous times for various prostitution, drug, and obscenity charges. At certain times, the club closed its doors, locked them up with the patrons inside, and the go-go dancers performed certain other services for the patrons—sometimes striptease, sometimes prostitution. Moreover, the dancers were expected to "entertain" Mickey as a part of their employment.

Delaine Grumman was one of his go-go dancers for a few months during 1976 and lived with him as well. She was well acquainted with the layout of his home. While working at his club, she was aware of narcotics sales being made. She was persuaded by Mickey to dance in the nude and claimed to have been coerced into performing acts of prostitution for some of the customers after hours. Soon, she discovered that McCann was dating five other women at the same time he was seeing her. Consequently, she refused to date two of his clients, and in revenge, she believes, Mickey set her up for a rape as punishment. Relations were broken off, both personally and professionally.

While working there, she had become acquainted with a frequent customer, Gary Lewingdon. He was at the club as much as four to five times a week. Soon, she began living with him at 62 North Pine Street in Newark, Ohio. Delaine sometimes woke up in the middle of the night screaming a fear of McCann—that he was coming to get her. She and Gary married on December 22, 1977—twelve days after the Forker's Cafe murders.

17

Gary and Delaine talked about their plans for two to three weeks before he and Charles took action. The two brothers began their surveillance of the McCann residence during the middle of January and, eventually, made three or four trips there. McCann's home at 4187 Ongaro Drive was located just inside I-270 in a suburban setting. On a quiet street lined with brick and stone ranch-style homes, Mickey's house was neatly tucked between two similar houses, as well as facing others directly across from it. The small backyard was fenced in, while the side yard contained the driveway and access to the large garage with two overhead doors. Neighbors on either side were no more than seventy-five feet away, and the houses across the street were nearly as close. The brothers, however, were not deterred by this proximity.

The house was U-shaped, with the front entrance in the middle of the resulting indentation. Delaine had carefully described the layout of the place, told them that his mother lived there with him, and gave them her description. She believed that he had a safe in his den where he kept most of his money. On their first trip there, they stayed outside for some two hours, watching Dorothy McCann watch television. They were aware of what time Mickey and Christine usually arrived home and from what direction. They located the phone wires to the house. On another trip, they tooled a vent pipe out of a basement window, trying to find an easy entry, but they couldn't get in.

The night of February 11–12, 1978, was another bitterly cold night with one-and-a-half feet of snow on the ground. Gary and Charles left the Pine Street house at approximately 11:00 p.m., as Gary said to Delaine, "We're going to Mickey's."

At Mickey McCann's well-kept home, his mother, Dorothy, was again at home alone. The two men parked Charles's car at a nursery this time—a short distance away directly at the end of Ongaro Drive. On previous trips, they had not parked there because it was on a heavily traveled, well-lit road, but on this particular night, it was well hidden because there were huge piles of snow on the side of the road where road crews had cleared the street. Somewhere around midnight, they walked boldly up the middle of the street to avoid leaving footprints in the deep snow, which McCann might see by his car headlights when he returned home in the small hours of the morning. They had planned to arrive long before that hour to take care of Mickey's mother and to search the house.

On arrival, they saw from the street through the living room windows that Dorothy McCann was again watching television. She was wearing a pink nightgown that tied in front and pink bedroom slippers. Moving around to the corner of the house, Gary cut the phone wires with the horse hoof nippers, or cutters, that he carried in a leather satchel, and then, both proceeded to the dining room entrance, leaving footprints in the snow as they went. Charles handed the Stoeger Luger to Gary and used a crowbar to pry open the patio doors to the dining room. The noise of the breaking door was quite excessive and brought Mrs. McCann to investigate. She looked around the corner from the living room door and saw Gary at the dining room entrance. At age seventy-seven, she was unable to move quickly but managed to reach midway to the front room before Gary got inside and opened fire, knocking over a dining room chair in the process. He shot her twice before his gun jammed. Dorothy backed up to the fireplace in the living room and fell. Gary handed the gun back to Charles, who took it to a small table there and unjammed it. He reloaded, dropping a few live rounds by the table, keeping his eye on the old woman. As he did so, blood was pooling by her body. Moving directly above her body, he fired point-blank into her head. In all, she had been shot three times around the right ear and once in the right shoulder. One shot had gone wild through the picture window. She died with one arm on the fireplace hearth, still wearing her pink slippers.

They searched without success for a safe, which Delaine had believed was hidden in the den. They looked for cracks in the paneling that might conceal a hinge but found none. Finally giving up the search for a safe, they searched the rest of the house for several hours. In Dorothy's bedroom, they found her purse which contained approximately sixty dollars. They ransacked the rooms, throwing clothing about and dumping drawers.

In Mickey and Christine's bedroom, they moved the mattress, took pictures off the walls, and completely tore up one picture, leaving the pieces on the bed. In a large dresser drawer, Gary found a .38 caliber revolver in a box and decided to keep it. He would use it shortly. They also found some Polaroid pictures—the homegrown variety of nude females. Gary carefully looked through them for pictures of his wife but found none. He kept the others.

In the basement, they ransacked a set of bookshelves and dislodged some of the suspended ceiling tiles. A bowl of change on the counter in the kitchen was pocketed. At one point during these long hours, Charles took off his gloves because they were cumbersome.

Gary walked around behind him, wiping off the fingerprints. "Put your damn gloves back on," he said.

Charles did.

Mickey was not yet home, so they waited. Gary found some nuts and began to absently crack them as he perused through the house, leaving the shells as he went. In the kitchen, Charles found some cereal and a can of Coke. He finished the cereal and left the bowl and spoon on the counter, along with the empty Coke can. One of the two, still cold from the short walk in the bitter cold, turned the furnace thermostat up to maximum, or ninety degrees.

Soon, Gary went to the corner bedroom where they could see the street. Charles returned to Dorothy's room where he lit his pipe and accidentally dropped his package of Sir Walter Raleigh tobacco on the floor. Later, he knocked the ashes in the floor. At approximately 3:00 or 4:00 a.m., they saw McCann coming in his red Cadillac, followed by Christine Herdman's light-green station wagon. They had intended to be in the garage as McCann arrived, but he pulled in too fast. As the cars pulled in the driveway and McCann pulled his into the garage, Gary and Charles ran to the kitchen where a garage entrance was located. Their hearts were pounding—they would have preferred to sneak up on an unsuspecting victim as they had on Dorothy.

Gary waited inside the door, gun ready and hand on the knob, for the sound of the screen door opening just outside then pulled open the inside door and stood back. Charles stood with his gun already pointed at the entrance. They knew two people were coming—Charles was to take the first and Gary anything after.

Christine opened the screen door as Gary pulled back the inside door. She backed up screaming as Charles nervously fired twice, hitting the Cadillac door and tire but missing Christine altogether. Charles told her to shut up, but she continued hysterically to scream. He fired again. Christine fell back into the garage, dead instantly. Her wounds were on the right side of her upper body to the forehead, face, and right shoulder.

Meanwhile, Gary had a grudge to repay and was after McCann. McCann saw what was happening and opened the door to the car. He was outside running through the snow—Gary firing McCann's own .38 four to five times from close behind. For whatever reason, he did not hit him. McCann was still running as Charles came around the corner and got him in the back with two shots. They dragged him back inside the garage, and Gary went over to make sure the girl was dead, while Charles took the clip out of the Stoeger Luger then replaced it. Gary went through her purse, the wooden handles bearing the impression of a bullet and found new dollars and a happy face key chain which he pocketed. Charles searched McCann, who was known to carry large amounts of cash.

Charles could see that Mickey was still breathing, but suddenly, McCann screamed, "Don't kill me. Don't kill me!"

Gary quickly came back, took the Stoeger Luger, and placed it in his mouth. He fired. He looked up as Gary shot him. His screaming stopped. Gary removed McCann's belt and lowered his trousers looking for a money belt. He raised his shirt and sweater, again finding nothing. He checked his pockets, dumping the contents on the garage floor—still nothing. Suddenly, they thought of the car. Wrapped in a package under the front seat of the car, they found two thousand dollars. They also located the garage door control and closed the double overhead doors. For all the shootings, only five shots had actually struck McCann—two in the back, two in the forehead, and one through the lip and into the roof of the mouth.

Again, they searched Christine. Possibly, she had stuffed some money into her slacks. Gary yanked them open, breaking the zipper. Underneath, she still wore her go-go dancer's bikini panties. Charles pulled up her shirt to see if she had hidden money in her bra but found she wore none. They went back to McCann and removed his shoes. This time, they found some—carefully wrapped in a sock stuffed inside one of the socks he wore. The sock yielded another seven to eight thousand dollars. They left with over ten thousand dollars at 5:00 a.m., again walking down the center of the street. It was still very cold, and a light snow was falling. The houses were all buttoned tightly, shutting out noise as well as cold. They could see a night-light on inside a neighbor's house as they passed.

At 6:30 a.m., they returned to Sixty-two North Pine Street.

Gary woke Delaine up to tell her the good news. "You don't have to worry about Mickey anymore."

She was extremely happy.

Jones

Jenkin T. Jones Jr.

FINANCES WERE IMPROVING IN the Lewingdon households. Charles finally had located a job at Dayton Precision in the Newark Industrial Park. In March of 1978, he used a thousand dollars of his share of the McCann money as a down payment on a new 1978 Ford pickup truck—black, with a silver band on the cab. There was a cap on the back, white, with wood-grain trim, and a row of distinctive amber lights jauntily topped the cab.

Gary made two purchases shortly after the McCann episode. He and Delaine purchased a house at 235 E. Main Street in Kirkersville, Ohio. It was small, only two bedrooms, but they were excited to have their first home and were planning some remodeling. For the second purchase, Delaine bought him an automatic Sturm Ruger .22 caliber using the name and address on her outdated driver's license—Delaine Grumman, 4104 Dundee, Columbus, Ohio. Gary took the gun to his workbench and, using a special tool, threaded the barrel to accept a homemade silencer. He also made one for Charles's Stoeger Luger. The silencers were identical and would fit either gun. When in place, however, the silencers blocked the sights, so Gary improvised a higher one that rose above the clumsy tubes.

The two brothers had developed a habit of cruising every Friday and Saturday night, looking for potential victims. After Charles got his job, however, he worked second shift and was not able to go out on Fridays. On Saturdays, his hours were shorter, noon to five in the afternoon, and he was free at night. Every Saturday, except for Christmas and New Year's eve, they scouted.

Jenkin Jones lived in a large, dilapidated mansion at 1036 Lancaster Road, just outside Granville, Ohio. Passersby often noticed the large pond and the workshop before they noticed the house, which appeared to have been pieced together of various cast-off materials. The house, covered with peeling, white shingles and adorned with many red shutters across its front, overlooked the busy highway. At age seventy-seven, Jones spent a great deal of his time in the shop where he ran a business of sharpening saws and repairing motors. At times, he even slept there on a cot, curled up with his dogs at his side. His business also took him to Rockwell Manufacturing in Columbus to buy parts for repairing tools. There, while Gary worked, Jones talked about his distrust of banks and often displayed large amounts of money.

They visited Jones's house once before to check it out. They saw the old man lying on the couch in the living room, watching television. In fact, Jones usually slept on the couch, having closed off the bedroom where he and his wife had slept when she was alive.

On April 8, 1978, they were to return. Earlier in the evening, Jones had gone to Columbus. His daughter, Doris Williams, and her husband, who both lived in the same house, regularly went to the Eagles Club in Buckeye Lake on Saturday nights. When they left at 8:00 p.m., Jones was not yet home.

Later that evening, at approximately 11:30 p.m., Lester Hulse, another son-in-law of Jones, passed by the house on his way home from work. He noticed a shiny, black, late-model Ford pickup truck parked along the highway across from and slightly past his father-in-law's house. In the flash of an oncoming car's lights, he saw what he thought to be a wood-grain finish on the cab of the truck, or an area of less shine. The amber lights glowed across its cab top. He continued on his way.

Jenkin Jones had returned from Columbus and was sitting in the living room in his favorite leather chair watching the evening news. Outside, the two men stealthily crept onto the huge concrete front porch. They peered in through the small panes of glass that lined the sides of the door and saw the old man sitting very close to the window.

Gary said, "You're going to have to shoot him right through the window."

Charles seemed unsure of what the bullet would do in that case and said, "I don't know whether I'll get him or not."

"Do it."

Charles opened fire. Splintering glass filled the air, and bullets crashed into the skull above the chair. The old man staggered to his feet, and Charles shot two more times. The two men broke the window and the storm door handle to get in, and Gary went to the man and fired two more times into his head. Bullets had pierced his left forehead, left back head, right back head, the base of his neck, and six inches below his neck on the back. As they entered the house, they took the phone off the hook.

Satisfied that he was dead, they began to search the house for hidden money—not an easy task as Jones had piles of material stacked in corners and covered with sheets and furniture piled up in corners. They tore open drawers, dumping the contents on the floor, and ransacked the entire house, upstairs and down. All of the upstairs rooms but one had obviously not been used for some time. Everything was covered with a thick layer of dust in those rooms, and they searched them only briefly. The one room which had been used, they covered thoroughly. Gary discovered two shotguns to his liking and moved them from one end of the house to another. He placed them in a chair there but never took them. Sometime during the search, the phone began to buzz as it does when left off the hook for some time. They replaced it in its cradle. They found some money hidden in a china closet, in a coin changer in a bedroom, and in a heat register in Jones's former bedroom.

In the basement, Gary discovered two dogs—one at each end of the house. Jones and his daughter owned six dogs, and only two were to survive the night. Outside, in a pen, were two German shepherds and a big collie tied to a chain, and indoors, he kept a Rat Terrier, a dachshund, and a Manchester. They shot two dogs in the basement to keep them from biting, but one escaped, running back upstairs past Charles, biting his boots as it passed. The man gave chase and shot at the animal in the kitchen but missed. Later, Jones's daughter would discover the dog shivering under the washing machine on the back porch.

By this time, they were ready to go outside to shoot the German shepherds in the pen by the shop and to search the old man's shop for money. Before they went outside, they grabbed Jones and pulled him toward the adjoining bedroom, out of sight of the highway. A large bloodstain marred the living room carpet where the body had lain. As they went, the rug at the doorway to the bedroom slid quietly inward under the body. The men checked his pockets for money, found a small amount, and then, unhooked his trousers and pulled them toward his ankles, expecting to find a money belt there. They tore open his shirt, sending buttons flying into the living room. Finally, they found a pocket road atlas that Jones carried with him. Inside its pages was some ten to twenty thousand dollars, only recently removed from a bank account.

Outside, they shot the two German shepherds but did not bother the collie. Behind the house, Gary noticed Jones's parked car and took a pump and an extension cord, which he saw inside the vehicle. Inside the shop, they searched some more but found nothing. They left for the truck, tossing Jones's keys to the ground beside the shop door as they did so.

They headed the truck toward Gary's new home in Kirkersville, ten or fifteen miles away. They split the cash equally. Gary pulled out a driver's license he had taken from Jones's pockets. He threw it out the window in Pataskala—where it was later found, pointing the direction of the escape route for the police.

At 1:00 p.m. on Sunday morning, Doris and her husband returned to the house. They noticed that all the lights were on, which was unusual, and that the kitchen and basement doors were both open. They couldn't find their little dog. They yelled for her father and, finally, discovered him at the door to his bedroom. Doris ran to the phone to call the emergency squad and her brother-in-law.

Meanwhile, Gary and Charles Lewingdon returned to Gary's house where Delaine was awakened so Charles could tell her what had happened. They showed her the money and the pump and extension cord that Gary had picked up during the search.

Later investigations would show that three of the bullets in Jones were from a Stoeger Luger .22 caliber semiautomatic pistol. The others were from a Sturm Ruger .22 caliber semiautomatic. Of the twenty-seven shell casings found at the residence, eighteen had come from the Stoeger Luger and eight of the remainder from the Sturm Ruger. The police knew that the same gun, the Stoeger Luger, had been used in the Forker's Cafe murders. But they would not tell the public.

WigWam

Gerald Fields

GARY HAD TAKEN TO constantly searching for new conquests on his way home from work. On one such trip, he noticed a group of buildings next to I-70. They were surrounded by a chain-link fence. His curiosity rose. He wanted to know what the place was. Maybe they would scout it on their Saturday excursion.

The Wigwam, 13645 Taylor Road in Fairfield County, is a club owned by the Wolfe family, who also owns the Columbus Dispatch, a TV station, one radio station, and half the other Columbus newspaper. The club is used to entertain business associates and guests and is located just between Interstate 70, near Pickerington, Ohio, and State Route 204—the first road inside Fairfield County at that point. The club has lavish entertainment facilities, including its own movie theater, several dining rooms, TV lounge, a bar, a large lounge for table games, a swimming pool, and several bunkhouses and cabins for overnight guests.

That spring, Rev. Gerry Fields was doing a member of his congregation a favor. The manager of the club, Fields's parishioner, had lost his night watchman, and Fields had volunteered to help out on Saturday nights only. On his first Saturday, the manager gave him a .38 Colt Special with a chip out of the handle to use on his rounds. It was Reverend Fields's practice to read his Bible and study during the long night in preparation for the Sunday morning service.

Just one week after the Jones's murder, Gary and Charles left their black truck parked right alongside the interstate and hopped the fence to the grounds. They were not prepared for an outing; they had no guns and did not wear their dark ski masks. They just wanted to find out what the hell it was. Once inside the fence, they crossed the field toward the buildings, passing some parked trucks as they went. One building they looked into held tractors and lawn mowers and was obviously a repair or maintenance shop. But that didn't tell them what the place was. They continued to one of the larger buildings where they saw a light. Looking through the window, they saw a man in guard's uniform, wearing a pistol, as he watched TV and read. They ran, frightened that they had come close to capture with no guns for assistance.

They returned the next Saturday for their second trip, but this time, they were forewarned about the watchman. They still wanted to know more about the place. This time, they watched the guard make his rounds, timing his trip as he checked in at every station, signing the time. His tour lasted approximately an hour.

The next Saturday was April 30, 1978, just three short weeks after Jenkin Jones was killed. Late Saturday night, two brothers wended their way from Gary's new home in Kirkersville, approximately ten miles away. This night, they used Gary's car rather than Charles's shiny black truck. They looked for a place to park just beyond the rear entrance of the club. Taylor Road dead-ended at the interstate, however, and a house sat directly at the end. They couldn't park there. Charles suggested they go round to the other side of I-70, to Route 40, and look for the same road name. There they found a spot locally known as Taylor Turnarounds, often used by teenagers as a lover's lane. Only two houses were located on this road, and they were not close to the far end by the freeway. Gary pulled straight in to the end, not worrying about turning the car around. It was approximately 11:30 or 12:00 p.m. as they ran quickly across the four-lane highway and crossed the fence.

Two sets of footprints left their scars on the wet, grassy field across to the rear entrance of the club. They waited behind a trough or tank for some time until they thought the watchman's rounds would be over. But, as they rounded a corner, there was the guard making his rounds, not following the same schedule of the week before. They ducked into a barn next to them, but the guard had seen them. He stopped next to a dump truck and fired a shot into the air.

"I know you are in there. I know you are out there."

The brothers saw only his shadow on the ground. They watched the arm raise and heard the shot. They ran outside, and both opened up on him—the Stoeger and the Sturm Ruger. Blood streaked the bed of the truck as Fields fell nearby. They moved cautiously toward the body. Gary, always fascinated by guns, picked up Fields's .38. As he did, the delicate trigger discharged the gun accidentally. They took his keys and flashlight to use in their search.

They left him there to die and began to search the buildings. The keys were unnecessary as the buildings were unlocked.

After searching several of the buildings, including the main WigWam, they heard a noise.

"What's that?" Gary said.

"It's him hollering," Charles replied, and they went back to finish him off.

Standing directly above his body, they fired at point-blank range four times into his temple and forehead. Satisfied, they dragged him to the alcove between the pump house for the swimming pool and a bunkhouse. As they went, his feet scraped up large amounts of mud. One of the brothers banged his head on a roof overhang, losing a black knit cap in the process. One vomited nearby. They turned his pockets inside out looking for money and dropped some change on the ground beneath the body. His wallet was pocketed for later perusal, while his glasses tumbled to the grass beside his body. The brothers left, using the same path by which they had entered.

As they again passed the big truck, Charles said, "I want to see if this thing would go through a car window head-on, through the glass, with a .22."

Charles fired—through the driver's window and through the windshield itself. The windshield absorbed and trapped both bullets.

Suddenly, Charles was anxious to leave. He looked at Gary, who still held Fields's flashlight and keys.

"Throw that shit down. Let's go," he said, and Gary flung them down by the truck.

They continued on their way, crossing the freeway on foot to the turnaround where they had left Gary's car. At the side of the pavement there, they looked through Fields's wallet on the trunk of Gary's car. They scattered papers around in the grass. They discarded his draft card, driver's license, and credit cards as they went. The only cash they found was one dollar. Disgusted, they tossed the wallet down as well and left it there expecting the impending rain to wash off any prints. Gary took the gun with the chip in the handle to his home in Kirkersville and put it in the basement with the rest of the weapons. This evening had been a farce—they had not intended to take the man tonight. They just wanted to satisfy their curiosity.

Hours later, on Sunday morning, a worried lady came to the rear entrance of the club, wondering why her husband had not yet come home. Mrs. Virginia Fields saw the dump truck with its shattered windows, bullets still embedded in the glass. She grabbed up the keys and flashlight lying there, realizing whose they were. She saw blood on the truck. Panic-stricken, she ran for the clubhouse, which she knew her husband used as a headquarters during the night, only to find the door locked and no answer from within. She ran again, falling in the leaves and mud in her panic, to a neighbor's house screaming for help.

When the sheriff's deputy arrived, he saw a woman in a brown outfit, sweatshirt, and mud and leaves on the front of her babbling about not being able to get her husband from the building and still carrying her husband's keys and flashlight. The deputy put her in his patrol car, called for a backup car on the radio, and went around to the groundskeeper's house in the rear. The groundskeeper said something was unusual—the chain-link fence was unlocked. They went inside, leaving Mrs. Fields in the car. Systematically, they began to follow Fields's rounds to see which stations he had checked into during the night. At one of the stations, they found a body, cold with rigor mortis, blood on the forehead. By walkie-talkie, the deputy requested the coroner and a detective squad.

At about the same time the body was being discovered, Daniel Bavard and his children were working their paper route. Taylor Turnaround being part of their route, he pulled to the end of the pavement while his children took the papers into the two houses on the street. Lying four to five feet from the side of the road were the discarded wallet and papers.

Mr. Bavard, a schoolteacher, said to his family, "There is something wrong here."

He picked up one of the plastic bags used to protect the papers from moisture and shoved his hand inside. Then he carefully picked up the wallet and other items with the covered hand and placed them in another newspaper bag. Thus protected, he laid the bag and its contents on the dash of his van and continued on the paper route.

Later that morning, Mr. Bavard went to the local authorities, the Reynoldsburg Police Department, to report that he had found a wallet. They said they would come to pick it up but never did. Gradually, he forgot about the wallet, and the children took the bag off to inspect the cards. The name read Gerald C. Fields.

Monday morning came, as it always does, and Daniel Bavard was in the bathroom shaving in preparation for school. When the radio news broadcast the murder of Reverend Fields at the WigWam, Mr. Bavard realized the significance of what he had found. He immediately called the Fairfield Sheriff's Office to tell them of his discovery.

The voice on the phone said to someone in the room with him, "We've finally got someone who knows something."

The deputy said someone would be out immediately for the wallet, a distance of some thirty miles.

Mr. Bavard said, "No, I teach two blocks from you. I'll bring it in."

However, the wallet was never checked for prints, even though Mr. Bavard offered to have his children's prints taken for comparison.

Early Sunday morning, when the brothers returned to Kirkersville, Gary told Delaine what happened.

"Well," she said, "he was shooting at you."

"No," said Gary, "he shot up in the air."

Martin

Jerry Martin, Martha Martin

GARY'S JOB AS A service repairman for Rockwell Manufacturing was located at 4560 Indianola Avenue in Columbus, five miles from Morse Road and State Route 161. It was this route, with access to I-270, which Gary often took home from work. At the northeast corner of Columbus, the crowded 161 suddenly becomes a beautiful, rural, residential area of expensive homes, well-manicured lawns, and heavy woods. Gary thought this looked like a very good prospective area for their next surveillance.

The next Saturday, they sat at the stoplight at the intersection of Morse and Sunbury Roads, where the change from business to residential occurs by a picturesque stream. On the southeast corner of this intersection, Gary noticed a long lane which exited way back to a store or some type of business. Gary wanted to find out what it was, but Charles was reluctant. There were a lot of cars back there, and Charles eventually talked him out of it. Instead, they parked at an abandoned farmhouse and walked through the woods. It was raining hard, and they almost got lost. Soon, they were soaked to the skin. Suddenly, the woods thinned, and they came across several houses. They looked over three which were together and finally decided on one as the most likely prospect. They were ready to go in when suddenly, a security light came on and frightened them away. They would try again next week.

The next Saturday was May 20, 1978, and the brothers parked their truck at 11:00 p.m., again at the abandoned farmhouse. They walked through a cornfield and followed a fence to the house at 3825 Morse Road. Inside, Mrs. Magdalena Schrenser, her husband, and her aunt and uncle were in the family room playing cards next to the triple-sliding glass door. Outside, the brothers watched. There were just too many people inside for them to handle, so they turned their attention to the house south of this one—across the two-hundred-acre field. They followed the fence line a ways, then crossed.

At 3823 Morse Road, Jerry Martin lay on the couch watching the late show. His wife, Martha, had already gone to bed for the night. Meanwhile, Gary and Charles were trying to find the phone wires outside. They found several wires—so many that they couldn't tell which was which. Gary pulled the rusty hoof nippers out of the leather satchel and cut one line which led to a tree. Charles found another one coming down a wall and cut it. Jerry Martin had an illegal phone, one he had wired himself, and it was this which caused their confusion. They moved back to the front windows of the house very quietly, peering in at Martin. They did not know who else was in the house or where they might be, so Gary moved around to what they thought was a bathroom window, expecting that possibly, the wife was in there. Charles stood at one of the double windows on the front porch and fired through the screen. At an inopportune moment, the silencer went bad and the Stoeger Luger let out a pretty good crack. The first shot got Martin in the leg, and he jumped up off the couch. Then Charles let him have it in the chest. Jerry Martin rolled forward to the floor.

Next door, Mrs. Schrenser's husband and uncle had gone to bed, pulling sliding glass doors shut and leaving the women in the family room to talk.

Around midnight, Magdalena's aunt said, "What is that noise?" as they heard four cracks, something like wood cracking.

"You don't have to worry around here. Nothing ever to pull our blinds."

Gary rushed around the house to where Charles stood at the front windows. He had heard someone get out of bed in the other room.

"Here she comes," he said.

That's when he took her, when she came through the door, firing three times right through the screen before his gun jammed.

Wearing dark pajamas, she was carrying a vase of dried flowers to protect herself with.

They went to the front door, finding to their surprise that the screen door was unlocked and the inside door stood open one-eighth of an inch. They went inside and immediately closed the shades, knocking over a red glass vase into a stainless-steel sink. As they did so, it made a tremendous racket. Gary went over to where Martin lay, grabbing Charles's Stoeger Luger as he went. He placed the gun against the top of the victim's head and fired, then to the back of his head and fired again. Powder burns surrounded the wounds. Jerry Martin had sustained a total of eleven bullet wounds.

They turned him over to search his pockets and found two hundred dollars in his wallet which they split. Gary took the hundred-dollar bill and stuffed it in his pocket. He threw the billfold down by the body and turned off the TV.

Next, they moved to the woman's body and ruffled up her clothes a little to check for hidden money—not likely as she was wearing her nightclothes. In the bedroom, on the headboard were two or three bank bags full of many denominations of coins. They took these, approximately six hundred dollars' worth. In another place, they found a brand-new pocketbook still in its bag, so they dumped the coins into it to carry them more easily. They found an old purse, but it was empty. They never did find the purse she was using, which was sitting next to the couch and contained $80.73. In what they at first thought was a utility room because the walls were unfinished, they found many clothes along the walls. They decided it was a room which was being remodeled as a walk-in closet. In there, Gary found a staple gun, which he liked. He put it in the satchel.

They were only in this house for twenty minutes to a half hour before they left, locking the doors behind them.

The next morning, Jerry and Martha Martin failed to pick up his mother at 10:00 a.m. as they had promised, and she was unable to reach them by phone. Worried, she called a daughter to ask her to check on them. She, in turn, sent her son, Albert W. Martin, or Jerry and Martha's nephew. He arrived around three-thirty that afternoon and checked around the grounds noticing nothing. There was no answer at the door, and it was locked. He looked in through the windows. The screens were torn, and the curtains were closed, but he thought he saw a hand lying upward on the floor and some blood. He immediately went next door to the neighbors and called the police.

He and the neighbor went back to the house where he asked the neighbor to look in and see if he saw the same thing. Shaken, he said he did.

After what seemed like an eternity, an officer arrived and also looked in the window. He saw nothing. Next, he looked in the door and did see something. He called his supervisor on the radio for permission to open the door. The supervisor said it would be better if the nephew, a relative, would kick it in. After a few tries, he did. He stepped one foot into the doorway and saw his uncle's body lying on the floor. The officer told him to wait outside, and he slumped to the step at the edge of the porch. The officer went in far enough to see a second body in the hallway. He turned around, pulled the door shut, and notified his sergeant that they had a double homicide.

Gary and Charles returned to Delaine and again she was told what happened. Charles took his worn-out silencer to the dump, about one mile from his house. He threw it in. He had trouble sleeping for a long while after this one.

Annick

Joseph Annick

THE STRAIN WAS BEGINNING to tell on Charles. His wife, Yvonne, knew nothing of his activities. To cover his weekend absences, he had asked Gary to tell her they were working together on maintenance jobs, and it was becoming more and more difficult to cover what he was doing. He had of late been spending more money than she thought was normal—buying a microwave oven, more and better furniture, and a new truck, all of which she was questioning. She was worried that he was gambling again as he had in Chicago. When questioned, her sister-in-law, Dee, told her that he was gambling and more—ominous words for Yvonne. Worse, Charles was not sleeping well at nights, often for weeks at a time.

Though there had been no murders since the Martins, they had scouted several places since then. In fact, Gary was constantly looking for places. Gary's trip home from work to Kirkersville took him over state route 310 from the interstate. Just north of 40 was a fairly new brick house with an orchard that they had looked at, as well as a white farmhouse on Route 16 that sat back off the road just at the edge of Pataskala. They also checked out a place just across from the Airstream camper dealer at the corner of 310 and 40 but decided that all of these were too populated for their needs. They were more wary now than when they had done McCann and were looking for isolation. The people in these houses had just narrowly escaped death and were blissfully unaware.

By the second or the third week of June, however, Charles said he had had enough. He couldn't take it anymore.

Gary was surprised, disappointed, and perhaps a little apprehensive that his brother had pulled out. Would he give away their secret now that he had had second thoughts? He tried to reenlist him. Sometime between the last of June and the first of July, he said, "You interested in starting up Saturday night again?"

"Nope." Nothing would sway him.

Pressure mounted on Dee and Gary now. Dee, believing that a strong offense is the best defense, went to a policeman in the tiny town of Kirkersville. She told Officer Wines that she knew who the .22 caliber killer was—that it was Charles. The officer made her repeat her story to his chief who, in turn, sent her to Lt Paul Short of the Licking County Sheriff's Office—a detective on the case who happened to live only a mile from Kirkersville. The story she told made no mention of her own husband in relation to the slayings. She told of Charles asking Gary to provide him with an alibi for the weekends, of Charles's unexplained purchases, of her problems with her former boss, Mickey McCann, and that McCann had forced her to "go out" with a Columbus police officer as a bribe to protect the bar from citations. Lieutenant Short checked out her story about the policeman. He could not verify any of it. In addition, he discovered that she had filed a previous complaint against her brother-in-law for supposedly starting a fire in her home and for his children's stealing some money from her house. Short figured she was a crank and filed away her statement to be forgotten.

Summer gave way to fall. Charles buried his Stoeger Luger on the farm—later regretted his action and couldn't remember where he had put it. With the help of a metal detector and many hours of searching, he finally retrieved it. He carefully oiled the surface and wrapped the gun in an oily bag stamped Rockwell Manufacturing from Gary's shop. He got an old toolbox and put his ammunition in the bottom. As he placed the gun on top, his thumb rested on the oily surface. He closed the lid of the box and placed it in a green utility trailer behind his house.

More months passed, more than six since the last murder. The police and the community were beginning to relax—perhaps the killer had left the area or something prevented him from continuing. An uneasy calm settled over Central Ohio. Unfortunately, it was again the Christmas season, and Gary was again in need of money. Why should he stop just because Charles had? After all, he had been the decision-maker anyway. Who needed his big brother? Much of the heat had died down, and the newspapers had lost interest in the story. There was nothing to worry about.

On December 5, 1978, Gary and Delaine left the children with a sitter and went out for the evening. They returned home later, and Gary went out again—this time carrying a leather satchel.

He went to an area unlike his other choices, except that it was also near I-70 in downtown Columbus. The area was a collection of older apartments and duplexes, crowded into several blocks. They were identical two-story dark-red brick with a single front entrance for each. In certain areas, clusters of white wood-frame garages were located for the residents' use. Gary waited in a garage across the street from 1064 Euclaire Avenue, Apartment A—the home of Joseph Annick and his sister, Anna. Mr. Annick was the assistant adjutant for the Ohio Department of the American Legion.

Gary did not enter the home this time, in a concession to the fact that he was alone. When the car pulled in, Gary opened fire. Annick was shot five times in the chest and stomach in the same brutal manner as the other crimes. But no Stoeger Luger this time, only the Sturm Ruger. Gary took what cash Annick had, then saw the credit cards. He took four from the wallet and left for home.

Annick's body would not be found until Tuesday morning by his sister.

Capture

Gary James Lewingdon
Delaine Lewingdon aka Grumain, Grummond
December 9, 1978

A FEW SHORT DAYS after the Annick murder, Gary Lewingdon brooded over the coming holidays. He wanted the children to have some nice presents. He fingered the credit card in his hand. Soon, he dialed the number for reporting stolen cards. The disinterested voice at the other end blandly told him that, yes, the card had already been reported stolen and that he had nothing to worry about. Gary thanked her and hung up. He debated. Was it worth the risk?

Later that evening, Gary and Delaine arrived at Great Southern shopping center in the far side of Columbus and successfully shopped at four different stores: Rink's, Kmart, Ontario, and Gold Circle. The clerks in those stores accepted the card without question. At the fifth store, Woolco, a young clerk named Cheryl Young collected the toys that the Lewingdons wanted to purchase, totaled the bill on the register, and checked the card number against her stolen card list. She hesitated and stepped back to consult with her supervisor. Nervously, Delaine attempted to grab back the card, then said she had to go back to the toy department for a minute. She circled the store and left.

Gary said, "I've been having a lot of trouble with this card."

Soon, he said he would check on his wife and also left the store.

The supervisor, realizing by their behavior that something was wrong, didn't want them to get away. Another young employee, Jeff

Slovak, went after them. He caught up with Gary as he reached his car.

Jeff said, "Would you like to come with me?"

Delaine was nowhere in sight.

Gary replied that he wouldn't. Slovak grabbed him, but Gary offered no resistance. They went back inside the store where a special duty policeman, who was working extra duty for the holidays, took over the prisoner. Officer Joseph Rich warned the man he was a Columbus police officer and was armed, but Lewingdon willingly cooperated. They soon discovered that Gary also had three other credit cards in Annick's name. The policeman recognized the name as a recent .22 caliber murder victim and realized the importance of this capture. While they waited, Gary wondered aloud how much his bond would be. He asked many times if he could take the car keys to his wife so she could go home. When the police arrived, Delaine and the car were already gone; she had her own set of car keys.

The officers placed Gary on the back of a paddy wagon. As they closed the door, he began sobbing—the kids would not get the toys he had bought for them. He also said his house needed insulation and the kids were cold.

Next morning, Sunday's papers carried bold headlines: *Caught!* They exclaimed and made sudden heroes of the young store clerks who had alertly made the capture. Ironically, this created a problem for Cheryl Young. She was a full-time student who had been secretly married eleven months earlier against the rules of her school. There was a possibility she would be expelled.

Downtown, the questioning soon began for Gary Lewingdon. That same night, he admitted involvement in the Annick slaying.

Meanwhile, Delaine was still free. Her first instincts were to hide the evidence. She went directly to Kirkersville to collect Gary's brown leather satchel. Inside were the incriminating .22 caliber Sturm Ruger used in several of the murders and Mickey McCann's .38. The satchel also contained a .22 caliber derringer, considerable ammunition, two ski masks, a pair of hoof nippers used for cutting wire, a pair of bolt cutters, a homemade silencer which fit the Sturm Ruger perfectly, and a pair of gloves. Poorly maintained, the guns were in bad shape and beginning to rust. She threw the satchel into the back of the cluttered station wagon in a large cardboard box and covered it with an old bedspread. She headed back toward Columbus. Leaving the car parked at 393 E. 18th Avenue, she spent the night around the corner at 1888 N. 4th Street—the duplex where Gary and Charles's mother lived. During the night, she hid Annick's wallet, containing his driver's license, in the bathroom, stuck behind a cabinet.

The next day, Sunday morning, December 10, 1978, was an anniversary of sorts. It was exactly one year from the date of the Forker's Cafe murders—the first of the series. After his initial interview by the police on Saturday, Gary had been placed in a cell for the night. He had by that time implicated his brother, Thaddeus Charles Lewingdon, in the same crimes. In addition, he had given directions for finding the weapon which he believed to be at his home, unaware that Delaine had moved them, but she had overlooked one—Gerald Fields's .38 caliber Colt with the chipped handle. That morning, police obtained a search warrant and began to search the house in Kirkersville at 6:30 a.m. Delaine, obviously, was not there, nor were most of the weapons. However, there was other damaging evidence, such as Fields's gun, which they found exactly where Gary had told them—buried beneath the workbench in the basement. They also found twenty-two targets and a two-by-four frame with shot marks in it as well as dents in the concrete wall behind and around it where bullets had missed or penetrated the boards. They found shell casings, which would eventually be matched to those in the Jones's and Fields's homicides. They found three other guns—all loaded but not implicated in any of the crimes. Upstairs were the bags of merchandise from the Columbus stores, containing receipts signed by the name Joseph Annick. There were also cancelled checks made out to Spitzer Dodge, which totaled $4,622 in payment for Gary's new car that he had purchased. They also found a brown billfold which they hoped was Annick's but was not. This evidence was important for two reasons: one, it was incriminating, and two, it substantiated at least part of Gary's statement and, therefore, tended to corroborate the rest—the involvement of his brother.

Sometime after the search was conducted, Delaine called the police department to learn what was happening to her husband. The detective, who knew that some of the weapons had not been located, casually asked where she was calling from. "North Fourth Street," she said, and a patrol car was dispatched while she was still on the phone. Although they hoped to catch her in the car with weapons, a mix-up occurred, and they arrested Dee at 3:50 p.m. as she was leaving the Fourth Street address—car keys in hand. The car was immediately located nearby and towed downtown to the crime lab.

Downtown, Dee was interviewed for approximately forty minutes, only in regard to her role in the use of Annick's credit card. The detective who interviewed her was unaware at that time of her connection to the .22 caliber case. He was only concerned with the Annick slaying. She was also given some time to talk with her husband, which encouraged him to later confess the crimes. By evening, the police had interviewed Gary twice, and he had admitted involvement in all ten of the slayings. At one point, he said that the Annick slaying didn't bother him. When asked if any of the others had bothered him, he didn't answer.

Eventually, Dee was charged with four counts of passing bad checks, offenses dating back to 1976. Later, she, too, implicated Charles in the slayings and, in addition, gave permission for a second search of her home for "property taken from the Jerry and Martha Martin homicide, regarding a purse and coins, etcetera." Four days later, this search took place, and a silver money changer taken from the Jenkin Jones residence and overlooked in the first search was found there in Delaine's dresser drawer, as well as various gun tools and homemade sights. Dee was soon released from jail and, eventually, all charges against her were dropped. Defense attorneys later contended that her role in the homicides was substantial and that a deal had been struck with the prosecutor, but she and the prosecutor staunchly denied this. However, she was never tried and remains free to this day.

Capture

Thaddeus Charles Lewingdon
December 10, 1978

BY LATE SUNDAY AFTERNOON, Columbus authorities were carefully laying the groundwork for the arrest of Charles—Gary's brother. Months earlier, the agencies involved in solving the cases had agreed that whichever department broke the case would have the first priority in arrest and detainment. Charles, however, lived in Licking County, out of the Columbus Police Department's jurisdiction. Obtaining a warrant for his arrest meant going to him in Licking County and detaining him in their jail. There was a way around this, however—if authorities could establish probable cause for the arrest, it could be done without a warrant, as long as the person was informed of the reason for his arrest. In laymen's language, probable cause means the police must have good reason to believe that the arrested person was the cause of the offense in question. There are some risks involved, as the court may later rule that the arrest was illegal and, therefore, any information obtained by, during, or after the arrest is not admissible in the trial.

By approximately 7:00 p.m. that Sunday, police had several sources of information on Charles—they had two interviews with Gary during which he implicated Charles, they had one with Delaine during which she also implicated him, they had one search of the Kirkersville house and one of the car where evidence was found that substantiated their statements. Police felt this constituted probable cause.

During that long afternoon and early evening of simultaneous interviews with Dee and Gary, Columbus police officials contacted

Licking County officials for assistance. Licking County sent Lt Paul Short out to locate and survey the layout of the rural home of Charles Lewingdon. Although it was already dark, he drove by. The house was a two-story, red frame structure on a hill set back from Ohio Route 668, about two miles south of I-70. It was located on an access road to Interstate 70, as were many of the homicides. The house, a faded, red-shingle affair, sat back a long, deserted lane behind a weed-filled field. The nearest neighbors were across the road and down a few hundred feet in either direction. A plan had to be developed to ensure the capture, and quickly. News media had already broadcast stories of Gary's arrest. Authorities feared that Charles might flee or destroy evidence. Also, both Dee and Gary had warned that he had access to arms and would resist arrest. Gary had even flatly stated that he would never be taken alive.

As these statements were still being taken, Columbus detectives were sent to a truck on I-70, approximately halfway to the farm-house, and were told to call in every half hour until they could be informed that probable cause had been established. They received that information sometime between 8:00 and 9:00 p.m. at the truck stop and radioed the Licking County Sheriff's Office to send assistance. The sheriff's office arranged to meet them at a state highway garage located at the intersection of 668 and I-70. For about an hour, officials assembled there and made plans for Lewingdon's capture. An assistant prosecutor from Licking County was present for witnessing the legality of the arrest. As commanding officer of the jurisdiction where the house was located, Sheriff Max Marston of Licking County took charge and coordinated the plans for the arrest. Six carloads of people finally completed the picture—three cruisers and two unmarked detective cars from the Licking County Sheriff's Office and one unmarked car from the Columbus Police Department.

By 10:30 p.m., they were ready to go. The cars pulled out in a specified order and proceeded to the farmhouse exactly two miles down the deserted country road. They roared some two hundred yards down the lane to the farmhouse and screeched to positions completely surrounding the house. Deputies and detectives ran heavily armed to assigned positions, "like SWAT in television but it was real life," as Lewingdon's wife would later say. Simultaneously, the telephone rang in the house. Sgt. Ike Predieri of the sheriff's office was on the phone to give instructions to Lewingdon. Inside the house, Charles; his wife, Yvonne; and his sister, Yelanda, were sitting around talking. Two sons were upstairs in bed.

"Is Thaddeus or Thaddeus Charles Lewingdon there?" said Sergeant Predieri.

"This is him speaking."

"You are surrounded. We have a warrant for your arrest. Give yourself up."

"I don't have any shoes or a coat on. Can I put them on?"

"Okay, you can get them on but come back to the phone so you get your instructions right."

Lewingdon did exactly as he was told. Outside, Sheriff Max Marston was on the bullhorn, also telling him to come out of the house and that he would not be harmed. There was no immediate response to this, except that lights came on in an upstairs bedroom. Shortly, one of the officers moved to the door on the screened-in porch at the rear of the house and knocked quite loudly. Another announcement on the bullhorn and the back door opened. Lewingdon appeared, coat and shoes on—the hands held high in the air. He was instantly surrounded by pushing deputies. Sheriff Marston patted him down for weapons and emptied his pockets, placing the contents on the ground where they stood. He was placed in a leather belt with hand-cuffs attached to the front, informed that he was under arrest, and read his rights according to the Miranda decision of the Supreme Court.

When things quieted down somewhat, he asked, "What's this all about?"

He was told that he was wanted as one of the .22 caliber killers, that his brother had confessed and implicated him. He replied that he had just minutes ago learned the news of his brother's arrest by a phone call from their mother. When told that he would be charged for these crimes, he replied that he hadn't killed anybody.

Meanwhile, other deputies rushed into the house to *secure* it, which in police parlance means "to assure its safety." The officials knew that two sons were living at home and had stories from Gary and Dee of the weapons that were at the house. They wanted to make sure that no surprises awaited them. No one asked permission to enter, but three or four officers did and searched the entire house for other people. They did not look for evidence, as they had no warrant to do so. Mrs. Yvonne Lewingdon stood paralyzed with fear in the kitchen as they entered.

"What's going on?" she asked.

"Your husband has been placed under arrest as one of the .22 caliber killers," she was told.

Shaken, she went outdoors and retrieved the items taken from Charles's pockets.

As they took him away to a waiting car, she shouted to her husband, "What can I do?"

"Get a lawyer," he replied—the only time he would mention an attorney for many hours.

Soon, the police, assured that no assailants awaited them inside the house, headed for Columbus with their prisoner. Sheriff Marston left two deputies at the house to prevent the removal of evidence. Later that night, Yelanda, Charles's sister, pulled out in her van. Deputies detained her and checked the clutter inside of the van for ten or fifteen minutes. It appeared that she had been living out of the van. No evidence was found, however, and she was allowed to leave.

Inside, Yvonne was tore up about what had happened. She was so shaken that she could not call a lawyer, but she did manage to call her sister, Victoria Adkins, for help. Later that night, after ascertaining that they were relatives of the lady of the house, they were allowed to pass. Victoria was also unable to contact a lawyer that night but finally managed to reach one by the next morning—many hours after Charles finished his taped confession.

Charles arrived in Columbus within the hour, having been read his rights both verbally and written—a total of four times. No attempt had been made to question him in the car on the trip back. After the paperwork and routine arrest procedures had been completed, Charles again asked what was going on, was again informed what the charges were, and that his brother was at that very moment telling everything he knew about the murders.

"Would you like to hear your brother while he gives his statement?"

"Yes."

He was taken to a closet-sized room which held the tape-recording equipment for the interview room next door. A small microphone was switched on in the room and the proceedings in the next room could be heard. Charles listened quietly for about ten minutes while Gary described the break-in at the Western Auto Store in detail. Twice, the detective asked him if he had heard enough. The second time, Charles replied that he had and that he would make a statement.

He added, "You better have a lot of paper and pencils—this is going to take a while."

The detective still had a major problem—they had not obtained the .22 caliber Stoeger Luger made famous in the killings. They believed it to be at the farmhouse. Bluffing, they told him they could easily get a search warrant and find the weapon themselves. Lewingdon, in order to prevent the upset to his family, signed a consent-to-search form and told them where to find the evidence they wanted so it would not be necessary to disturb his family further. He laughingly added as he signed the form that they could search the place for twenty years and never find it. He himself had buried the gun at one time and had later spent three days with a metal detector trying to find it himself.

The detective weakly replied, "Is that so?"

Once during the long night, he asked if he could be executed for the crimes.

Back in Licking County, the two deputies were again joined by several Columbus detectives who gave them the consent-to-search form—the officers executed the search according to Lewingdon's instructions. In a green utility trailer behind the house, they found a green ammunition box containing a .38 caliber revolver and three trigger guards or locks; four boxes of .22 caliber long rifle ammunition; two boxes of Winchester .38 caliber ammunition; three

.22 caliber clips for the Stoeger Luger; and the Stoeger Luger with Lewingdon's thumbprint clearly imbedded in the oily surface. In his pickup truck glove compartment was a .25 caliber automatic pistol. These guns displayed no signs of rust and were well maintained. All had been stolen from the Western Auto Store in Columbus the previous year.

On Monday morning, December 11, both brothers were arraigned and held without bond in the Franklin County jail. Gary was declared indigent, and a public defender was appointed for him. A separate attorney was appointed for Charles, since both brothers had implicated the other as the instigator of the crimes.

A long year was over for the people of Central Ohio.

Family Background

Material excerpted from the Columbus Citizen-Journal
December 12 and 14, 1978, and January 26–27, 1979

Thaddeus Charles Lewingdon was born on December 22, 1936, to Florence May Jeffries Lewingdon and Joseph Lewingdon Sr. He was the fifth child of this couple and was born at home. His father was a foreman in a mattress factory.

Three years later at 5:50 a.m. in February 1940, the sixth child, Gary James Lewingdon, was born, also at home. Sometime later, his official birthday was changed to February 14, 1940.

Both boys were in Columbus, Ohio, but later moved to Proctorville, Ohio—a river town across from Huntington, West Virginia. Gary entered the first grade in this town and completed the eighth grade here. Then, the Lewingdons moved to Chesapeake where Gary eventually graduated from high school. Friends from school remember both boys as loners, quiet, and shy. Charles dropped out of school in 1953 at the end of his sophomore year, at age sixteen. Possibly, he joined the army at that time. It is known that he served at least six months in the army before being undesirably discharged for going AWOL. Army officials discount this, however, since at that time, he would have had to be seventeen to join and would have to have his parents' permission. In school, Charles had been a *B* student until eighth to tenth grades when his grades began to drop.

On March 12, 1955, at age eighteen, Charles married Linda Jane Harshbarger, who was then fifteen years old. They were divorced the next year, and she retained custody of their son, Robert Eugene Lewingdon.

After graduation, Gary joined the Air Force where he went to technical school in hydraulics and rose to the rank of airman second class. After being discharged in 1962, he worked two years for Black and Decker and then thirteen years for Rockwell Manufacturing as a service repairman, where he was still employed at the time of his arrest.

Charles remarried in 1959 or 1960 and dropped out of sight in Chesapeake. Both brothers were members of a local Lawrence County club, which built flying model airplanes. Charles was fairly good at it. At about this same time, their father had a stroke, and Charles took over his job as a foreman at the mattress factory, but he only stayed a month or so. Joseph Lewingdon Sr. was admitted to the Veteran's Administration Hospital on October 14, 1959, and was there off and on until he was permanently discharged in May 1960. He and his wife returned to Columbus, Ohio, for his retirement.

By that time, Charles had gone to Chicago. He worked as a machinist there and married for the third and final time. Her name was Yvonne Jane Sexton, and she was from Logan County, West Virginia. Their first child was born in Chicago in April of 1960—a boy who they named Thaddeus Charles Lewingdon Jr. The second was born in West Hamlin, West Virginia, on

Christmas Eve of 1961. They stated that Yvonne had received her prenatal care in Chicago. It is unclear why they were there, but it may have been for a holiday visit to friends.

Their father died in 1963 after Gary had been discharged and returned to Columbus where his parents lived. Gary moved in with his mother in her North Fourth Street duplex, where he stayed for fifteen years. In 1977, he moved in with a girlfriend, Delaine Louise Grumman, on North Pine Street in Newark, Ohio, and married her on December 22, 1977. Her three children by two previous marriages lived with them—Mary, Yvonne, and Eddie. Delaine was a CETA worker in Newark and was studying to be a nurse at the time of the arrests.

Shortly after his father's death, Charles also returned to Columbus with his family. Soon, his third child was born—Rodney Allen. In the summer of 1974, he again returned to Chicago, but when he was injured on the job, he came back to Licking County, Glenford, Ohio, where his children enrolled in Glenford schools. He lived in a rented rundown farmhouse with his wife and two sons—the oldest having gone to the service. The family raised chickens and sold eggs. After returning to the area, he had difficulty finding a job and, for a time, was on welfare. Eventually, he found a job at Dayton Precision in the Newark Industrial Park and stayed approximately a year. On November 20, 1978, he again changed jobs and went to work for Columbus Steel Drum in Blacklick, Ohio, where he was employed when he was arrested, only twenty days later. There he was rated as an ideal employee. He was slated for a management training program when arrested.

Charles had no arrest record and claimed he didn't drink. Gary, on the other hand, had spent several nights a week at a bar where he met his wife and had an arrest record of three misdemeanors—suspicious person, intoxication, and carrying a weapon.

Perhaps the most chilling part of the brothers' story is the family tendency toward violence. Other family members have been arrested on such charges as armed robbery, rape, kidnapping, and vehicular homicide. Several family members are in prison. Joseph Lewingdon Jr., Charles's and Gary's nephew, has been arrested for vehicular homicide and is a construction worker with self-done tattoos. His brother is already in prison. According to Joseph, the family does not get along but are "close in our own way." Ann, Joseph's sister, says she is sorry for her grandmother, Gary and Charles's mother. "Grandma, she is really a nice lady."

Causative Factors

PSYCHOLOGISTS HAVE BEEN ABLE to identify some common characteristics of murderers. Obviously, they, at most times, look and behave like ordinary men; otherwise, if they somehow resembled the popular image of a murderer, they would be identified and put under restraint before they could do any harm (Brophy, 248). In some cases, however, acquaintances of these people have, with hindsight, managed to identify an unusual expression of, perhaps, extreme hatred or brutality which, at that time, puzzled them but later gained alarming significance. Ted Bundy, the law student convicted of murdering many young look-alike women, was reported to at times demonstrate a sudden, bone-chilling flash of dementia in his facial expression (Rule, 103).

Dr. David Abrahamsen, well-known forensic psychologist, identifies the following as predominant characteristics of the murderer:

1. Extreme feelings of revenge and fantasies of grandiose accomplishments, which may result in the acting out of hateful impulses.
2. Loneliness, withdrawal, feelings of distrust, helplessness, fears, insignificance, loss of self-esteem.
3. Sexually overstimulating family situation.
4. Errors of spelling or speech related to emotional disturbance in early childhood.
5. Tendency toward transforming identification; blurred self-image; suggestible, impressionable.
6. Inability to withstand frustration and to find sufficient gratification for expressing hostile, aggressive feelings through constructive outlets.

7. Inability to change persistent egocentricity or self-centeredness into elements of healthy ideals and conscience—resulting in dependency on and contempt for authority.
8. Suicidal tendencies with depression.
9. Seeing the victim as the composite picture of the murderer's self-image.
10. History of previous antisocial or criminal acts associated with threatening or committing murder.

(Abrahamsen, 28–29)

Obviously, not all people who exhibit the above tendencies are murderers. It is by the act of murder that one becomes a murderer, and many who carry the above traits may never commit the act. What is the line that separates those who do from those who don't? Some suggest that the economically and socially underprivileged strata of our society produces the greatest number of these offenders. "Almost without exception, one finds in their early backgrounds not only economic want, but cruelties and miseries of every kind. Such early conditioning predisposes to a marked undervaluation of life" (Wolfgang, 120).

A brief case history that illustrates this theory is that of Herman D., age twenty-one, who, while holding up a milk truck in broad daylight, shot and killed the driver when he offered resistance. Herman had been a serious behavior problem as early as age six when he was expelled from kindergarten. Although he came from a well-established family, his father was a selfish athlete who didn't want a child, so his wife tricked him into pregnancy. The father beat the boy and burned his fingers when he stole at age three. Herman loved his mother, and they often slept holding hands when the father was away. The mother threatened suicide if the boy did not straighten up. Once, she even slashed her wrists and locked herself in the bathroom to die. Herman, still a child, broke down the door, applied a tourniquet, and saved her life.

Later, he ran away, climbed telephone poles, had temper tantrums, and even set fire to his own clothes. When his uncle once refused him entry to his house, Herman exhibited other violence toward animals—cutting turtles in half with a hatchet and once put out the eye of his Airedale with a dart.

He bullied his friends, who were usually his social inferiors. He was expelled several times but had a good IQ (Wolfgang, 126).

Herman would be considered a sociopath by psychologists. The *sociopath* is "one who exhibits none of the anxiety or self-concern of the psychoneurotic and none of the bizarre behavior of the psychotic and is characterized by a lack of emotions and remorse" (Hahn, ix).

A second type of murderer is the *psychopath*, who experiences a complete break with reality (Abrahamsen, 11–12). An example of this type would be the infamous Son of Sam murderer who believed that his neighbor's dog, Sam, gave him his instructions to kill. Until he followed the dog's orders, he could not sleep. The Yorkshire Ripper, who regularly killed his victims by stabbing them repeatedly in the abdomen, was himself the victim of an overpowering hatred of women. His own wife, who was unable to bear children, he placed on a pedestal, far above the women of the night whom he victimized. Psychologists believe he was expressing his resentment of their child-bearing ability (Yallop, 301).

Another example of this type is the typical assassin of public figures. Dr. Abrahamsen has done an intensive study of eleven defendants charged with threatening the president or other government officials and compared them with Lee Harvey Oswald, James Earl Ray, Sirhan Bishara Sirhan, and Arthur Herman Bremer (who was convicted for the shooting of Governor George C. Wallace). All of these men showed surprising similarities in their family backgrounds, their personalities, and their behavior patterns. This was also true of the killers of Presidents Lincoln, Garfield, and McKinley.

> The actual or would-be assassins displayed intense and recurrent fantasies of revenge and omnipotence which stimulated their violent impulses into action. Highly characteristic was their personal failure, another expression of the loss of self-esteem so prevalent in murderers—all of the real or would-be assassins grew up in a family

where there was poverty, hostility, quarreling, and fights; absent, unassuming, or neglectful fathers, and domineering mothers. (Abrahamsen, 18)

Dr. Abrahamsen also notes these particulars:

- *Lee Harvey Oswald*—his father died before Lee was born. He was raised by a domineering, protective mother.
- *James Earl Ray and Sirhan Sirhan*—their fathers struck or beat their sons, and both fathers left their families.
- Arthur Bremer—his father drank heavily; there were fights in the home; his mother was disorganized, probably mentally ill, and, at times, refused to cook for the family and locked her husband out of the home.

Unsatisfactory relations with women were exhibited by Oswald, Ray, Sirhan, and Bremer. Oswald's wife says he was impotent. All were loners—the child who cannot trust his parents trusts other people. They had antisocial criminal records and histories of mental disturbances. All performed poorly in school and had frequent absences. They tended to exhibit an inability to distinguish between reality and fantasy. John Wilkes Booth (Lincoln's murderer), for example, was another famous assassin—Oswald thought he would be a hero in Russia when he went there; Sirhan wanted to be a diplomat but couldn't complete college, so he decided to be a jockey where he suffered a concussion in a fall from a horse; Bremer fantasized about being a great photographer or writer (Abrahamsen, 19–22).

Dr. Abrahamsen also noted that persons charged with violent crimes usually demonstrated good grades in school, except in spelling. He cites some sample spelling errors found in Lee Harvey Oswald's historic diary:

complusery for compulsory
kicten for kitchen
yonuge for young
exalant for excellent

> *tehniction* for technician
> *sptacular* for spectacular
> *divocied* for divorced
> *oppossition* for opposition
> *enviorments* for environments
> *permonet* for permanent
> *admiriers* for admirers
> *habituatated* for habituated
> *quiality* for quality
> *patrioct* for patriotic
> (Abrahamsen, 27)

Although these facts are interesting, they are obviously not helpful in identification of potential murderers, as they are characteristics of an extremely wide segment of today's society.

The most recent example of a psychotic assassin was the attempt of President Reagan's life by a man who thought he did it for the love of a teenaged movie actress.

A third type of murderer is the *nonpsychotic*—by far the most numerous. This individual exhibits no psychological disorder that can be identified. Rather, life and death seem unimportant to him, and he kills "as easily as children in their play" (Wolfgang, 120). This individual does not seem to realize the deprivation which he imposes on his victim; his killing is rational and consciously acceptable to him (Abrahamsen, 11–12). Murders, such as the barroom brawl, the family argument, or jealous lover would fall into this category usually. It is also in this category that we encounter the role of the victim. Only one-fifth of the victims of homicides were unknown to the killer up to a few hours before death (Brophy, 128–129). In other words, only 20 percent are random assaults. Most murderers know their victims, and therefore, sometimes the victims can play an unwitting or even conscious role in their own deaths. While no one deserves to die, some, by provocation, abuse, startling a housebreaker unintentionally, screaming or panicking, being promiscuous, associating with shady characters, or even by being the first to resort to violence, are active, instrumental precipitators of their own demise (Wolfgang,

24). This is certainly not to alleviate the guilt of the offender. The law does not recognize any excuse for capital acts except that of self-defense or insanity. In all other cases, man is expected to show restraint, even to the point of allowing a burglar to make off with his property. In the eyes of the law, a man's life is worth more than a possession. To summarize, "the homicide 'out of the blue' in which the victim is struck down without reacting in any way, is extremely rare" (Wolfgang, 70). Almost invariably, there are words or actions, however legitimate and approved by society at large, which provoke the killer into the use of force.

In addition to the psychological traits of the offenders, there are certain sociological characteristics of the homicides themselves which can serve to shed some light to our discussion of homicides. For example, both murderer and victim are usually of the same race; if Negro, the slaying is usually done with a knife, while if white, it is usually done by a beating on a public street (Wolfgang, 15). A high proportion of killers have a previous arrest record, most usually of a type against the person rather than against property (Wolfgang, 22). Most murderers have been shown to have a lower IQ than offenders against property and certainly lower than the general population (Wolfgang, 9). Young males predominate in the role of killers, usually in their early thirties or younger, with many in the late teens. Very violent crimes are rarely committed by children under fourteen or by persons over forty (Wolfgang, 4). This applies to victims as well. In murders committed in 1980, 9 percent were of victims aged fifteen to nineteen, 17 percent aged twenty to twenty-four, 17 percent aged twenty-five to twenty-nine, and 13 percent aged thirty to thirty-four (US Department of Justice, 369). The actual number of arrests per one hundred thousand inhabitants in the north central region of the United States has fluctuated over the decade of the seventies, with no discernable pattern except for a slight increase in the time of economic recession:

1970	8.7
1971	8.8
1972	7.8

1973	7.0
1974	10.2
1975	6.9
1976	6.4
1977	7.8
1978	7.3
1979	9.1
1980	7.5

(US Department of Justice, 416)

From 1964 to 1980, the total number of murders and nonnegligent manslaughters has nearly tripled:

1964	7,990
1965	8,773
1966	9,552
1967	11,114
1968	12,503
1969	13,575
1970	13,649
1971	16,183
1972	15,832
1973	17,123
1974	18,632
1975	18,642
1976	16,605
1977	18,033
1978	18,714

| 1979 | 20,591 |
| 1980 | 21,860 |

(US Department of Justice, 367)

During these years, the use of firearms accounted for an average of approximately 60 percent of the weapons or methods used in these crimes (US Department of Justice, 367).

Social class carries a marked weight in the predetermination toward violence. Whereas the higher classes are more likely to commit suicide, the lower classes are more likely to commit homicide (Wolfgang, 5). The subculture of violence that exists in some sections of the lower class deeply ingrains the response of violence and may even produce guilt if it is avoided. Although Negroes commonly show a rate four to five times that of whites for assaultive crimes, this is primarily due to a cultural bias rather than a genetic or biological tendency toward violence (Wolfgang, 8). Studies done in Minnesota with six convicted murderers and their parents led to the conclusion that child abuse had been a constant experience, far beyond the ordinary bounds of discipline (Wolfgang, 201). Thus it may be that violence is first learned through a victim's eyes.

In cases where there are two or more offenders, the role of dominance becomes apparent. Crime is a way of asserting dominance, and the history of crime is full of relationships between high and medium dominant personalities (*Crimes and Punishment*, 14). One in every twenty people in the general population have dominant personalities; this number is the same in the animal kingdom as well (*Crimes and Punishment*, 9). A knowledge of the role of dominance was used quite effectively by the Koreans in their prisoner of war camps during the Korean War, when they were able to prevent all escape attempts by American prisoners by analyzing dominance traits. The Koreans observed the Americans long enough to determine who were the dominant or leader figures. These were removed and placed under heavy guard. The others became far easier to handle and could even be left with almost no guard at all (*Crimes and Punishment*, 11).

In a study done by John B. Calhoun at the National Institute of Mental Health, rats were placed in conditions of overcrowding. Of those rats, the dominant 5 percent quickly became a criminal 5 percent. These criminal rats raped females and became cannibalistic (*Crimes and Punishment*, 12)

A classic case of the role of dominance in homicide is the famous relationship of Nathan Leopold and Richard Loeb. Both boys were highly intelligent sons of very rich families. As an intellectual challenge to alleviate their boredom, they kidnapped and murdered a young acquaintance. Together, they dreamed of themselves as supermen destined for greatness. Nathan Leopold, a homely boy, idolized his handsome friend Richard Loeb and would do anything to please him. According to a college friend, Loeb "was handsome, athletic, a ladies' man, but beneath that exterior arrogant and sadistic, his sick mind could concentrate only on the discussion of crime. Leopold, unlike Loeb, was a quiet, studious, serious, very gentle boy" (Gertz, 17). Leopold was dependent to Loeb. A famous crime writer of the day felt that the two were equally guilty, that neither boy alone would have killed anyone, and that it was the "peculiar combination of their characters, which, acting together, produced the murder" (Gertz, 64). This relationship led to the death of young Robert Franks, their victim, the eventual death of Loeb in prison, and thirty-four years for Leopold in prison before parole (Brophy, 217).

Finally, let us look at the common motives for homicide. There are five police-recorded motives which are involved in eight out of ten cases—a vaguely defined altercation, domestic quarrel, jealousy, argument over money, and robbery (Wolfgang, 23). "In thirty-two cases involving fifty-seven offenders and six victims, a felony, in addition to the killing, was perpetrated at the time of the slaying. In most cases, the other felony was robbery, and white males accounted for a larger proportion of these felony-murders than they did among all homicides in general" (Wolfgang, 24).

Conclusions

GARY AND CHARLES LEWINGDON are both white males, somewhat over the average age for murderers. Charles was forty-two at the time of his arrest, and Gary was thirty-eight. It is rare for a murderer to be over forty. They were considered loners by their friends in school. They did both show an interest in the model flying club, however, and became somewhat proficient in it. This was probably what encouraged Gary to join the Air Force later. They were both experiencing financial difficulties at the time of the crimes—Charles being on welfare and Gary taking on a wife and three children. Both situations would be stressful.

The question of dominance is an interesting one in this case. Psychiatrists claim that an impressionable person is more likely to commit murder than one who is not (Abrahamsen, 28–29). Although both brothers later claimed that they were encouraged by the other to commit the crimes, it seems to me that Gary was probably the most suggestible. Delaine, in fact, was quoted as saying that he was very easily led by others. While she blamed Charles as his mentor, I think the facts show otherwise—the first murder occurred two blocks from her home and only twelve days before their marriage; she was fully informed of each crime, if not before then at least after; the last murder occurred the same evening that she and Gary had gone out and was shortly before Christmas like the first; one murder was of her previous boss against whom she held a grudge; and when Gary was finally arrested, it was her children's presents for Christmas which were on his mind. It seems to me that it was Delaine, not Charles, who held great influence over Gary and encouraged him in these endeavors. That Charles was the less motivated of the two is shown in his reluctance to continue; it is also obvious from the location of the crimes near Charles's house or on his way home from work, with the exception of Mickey McCann's, in which case, the motive was clear. In addition, Gary had shown throughout his life that he was more goal-oriented than his older brother. Gary held a job longer, finished high school, and was honorably discharged from the service. Charles tended more to give up—he dropped out of school, ran away from the service, divorced twice, and was likely to quit his jobs frequently, though he showed talent in his work. In fact, the only thing he did show tenacity in was his third marriage, which had lasted approximately twenty-three years at the time of his arrest and had produced three sons. Charles also had associated with known criminals in Chicago, according to Delaine, which may have had an influence on his later activities.

As in many such cases, both brothers held a job during this year of vicious bloodshed and evidently gave no hint of their weekend activities to their fellow workers. In addition, Delaine was actually in nurse's training at that time—learning to care for others while being paid by the federal government for retraining. Their total lack of remorse or emotion during these crimes, their totally non-bizarre behavior otherwise, and their unconcern for society's mores marks them as sociopaths. Gary, however, pleaded "not guilty by reason of insanity" and is now serving his time in the Lima State Hospital for the criminally insane. Charles was found guilty and is currently serving his sentence in the Lucasville penitentiary of Ohio.

Many murderers carry a previous record, most likely for assaultive charges. Gary did have a record but only for misdemeanors, and Charles had no previous record at all.

One theory regarding murderers is that they come from a subculture of violence (Wolfgang). The Lewingdon family fits this description—with several members serving or having served time in prison on charges of varying degrees of violence. The lack of concern for human life and/or welfare is apparent here and, typically, is transmitted through the family. In addition, some studies have determined that murderers have themselves often suffered child abuse. We have no evidence on this point regarding the Lewingdons.

These crimes occurred during hard economic times of inflation and unemployment. This would fit the pattern of murders nationwide when a sharp increase occurred during 1979. The vast majority nationwide are committed by firearms, as were these. Also, the lower social class is far more likely to commit homicide than others. Gary and Charles both lived in poverty conditions.

Of the ten victims in these crimes, probably fully half could be said to have played a role in their own deaths. The Forker's Cafe murders were random choices for robbery only, as were Annick and Martin. Also, the victims could not be shown to have affected the outcome of the other victims. However, Jenkin Jones led somewhat of an eccentric life and carried that into his handling of finances. He imprudently carried large amounts of cash with him and even more imprudently made that fact known in his travels around the area. He spoke once where the wrong man could hear. Mickey McCann obviously was living on borrowed time. He was associating with syndicate, drug dealers, and prostitutes. He was repeatedly being raided by the police but persisted in breaking the law. He was a pimp according to Delaine. He forced girls into prostitution against their will and took revenge if they did not cooperate. These activities are not conducive of friendships. He also carried a firearm to let it be known. According to police, it was common knowledge on the entire west side of Columbus. He dated many women, and all were probably aware of these habits. Christine Herdman, by her relationship to McCann, was risking her own safety. She also associated with unsavory people and probably performed illegal acts with or for them. Her scream of terror when she saw the intruder probably ensured her death, though the brothers were not likely to show any mercy regardless. In other situations, a scream might mean the difference between life and death for a victim of a crime. Dorothy McCann's only error was in living with her son. Gerald Fields had accepted a job for which he was unqualified—as a night watchman at an expensive club. Someone trained in police work might have escaped with his life since the brothers actually intended no harm that night. Once the discovery was made, however, his death was sealed.

The motive in every case was robbery, although Mickey McCann served to satisfy some jealousy on Gary's part and revenge for a previous disagreement with Delaine. Both motives are in the top five police-recorded motives for homicide. In his sentencing of Charles

Lewingdon, Judge Wright of Mansfield, Ohio, in an apt summary, stated, "Sir, you have been found guilty of six execution-style killings with the only apparent motive being profit. No signs of mercy were shown."

Bibliography

"Criminally Insane: Turned Loose Too Soon?" US News & World Report, *Vol 94, No. 25.* US News & World Report Inc., June 27, 1983, pp 52–55.

1980 Census of Population and Housing. US Department of Commerce, Bureau of the Census.

Abrahamsen, David, MD. *The Murdering Mind.* New York: Harper & Row, 1973.

Bailey, F. Lee. *For the Defense.* Atheneum, New York, 1975.

Balchin, Nigel. *Fatal Fascination.* Boston: Little, Brown and Company, 1964.

Biggs, John Jr. *The Guilty Mind: Psychiatry and the Law of Homicide.* New York: Harcourt, Brace and Co., 1955.

Brophy, John. *The Meaning of Murder.* New York: Thomas Y. Crowell Co., 1966.

Capote, Truman. *In Cold Blood.* New York: Random House, 1965.

Clark, William A. *The Girl on the Volkswagen Floor.* New York: Harper and Row, 1971.

Crimes and Punishment: A Pictorial Encyclopedia of Aberrant Behavior, Vol 1. BPC Publishing Ltd. and Credit Services, 1973.

Fairfield County: Clerk of Courts, Change of Venue Hearing.

Gertz, Elmer. *A Handful of Clients.* Chicago: Follett Publishing Co., 1965.

Hahn, Jon K., and Harold C. McKenny. *Legally Sane.* Chicago: Henry Regnery Co., 1972.

Kendall, Elizabeth. *The Phantom Prince: My Life with Ted Bundy.* Seattle: Madrona Publishers, 1981.

Klausner, Lawrence D. *Son of Sam.* New York: McGraw-Hill Book Co., 1981.

Newark Advocate. Newark, Ohio: Advocate Printing Co.

Olsen, Jack. *The Man with the Candy: The Story of the Houston Mass Murders*. New York: Simon and Schuster, 1974.

Rule, Ann. *The Stranger Beside Me*. W. W. Norton & Company. New York, 1980.

Sanders, Bruce. *The Telltale Corpus Delecti*. New York: A. S. Barnes and Co., 1966.

Smith, Edgar. *Brief Against Death: Written in his Eleventh Year on Death Row*. New York: Alfred A. Knopf Co., 1968.

Sparrow, Gerald. *Women Who Murder*. London: Abelard-Schuman, 1970.

The Columbus Citizen-Journal. Columbus, Ohio.

Transcript of Proceedings, Transcript of Motion to Suppress Hearing, State of Ohio vs Thaddeus Charles Lewingdon. Richland County: Clerk of Courts.

Transcription of Proceedings, State of Ohio vs Thaddeus Charles Lewingdon. Licking County: Clerk of Courts.

Trilling, Diana. *Mrs. Harris: The Death of the Scarsdale Diet Doctor*. New York: Harcourt, Brace, Jovanovich, 1981.

US Department of Justice, Sourcebook of Criminal Justice 1982. Albany, New York: The Michael J. Hinterland Criminal Justice Research Center, 1983.

Wolfgang, Marvin, Ed. *Studies in Homicide*. New York: Harper and Row.

Yallop, David A. *Deliver Us from Evil*. New York:Coward, McCann, and Geoghegan, 1982.

Zerman, Melvyn Bernard. *Call the Final Witness: The People vs Darrell R. Mathes as Seen by the Eleventh Juror*. New York: Harper and Row, 1977.

C.   52 N. Pine St., two blocks away from Forker's Cafe,
where Gary Lewingdon and Dee Grumman lived

D.   Tire garage: Gary and Charles hid behind a stack
of tires as Forker customers left the parking lot; their
car lights passed over the brothers' hiding place.

A. Forker's Cafe at the right, and a tire company across the side street

B. The porch and steps at the rear of the café—where two women died

A. Front entrance to McCann's house

B. View of the proximity of the neighbor's house

C. View of McCann's garage from the neighbor's yard

A. View of Jones's house and shop—taken from the position where Charles's truck was parked on the night of the murder

B. View of Jones's front porch and small windowpanes by the front door, through which the Lewingdons shot Jones

A. Taylor Turnarounds—the Lewingdons parked here, crossed the fence
at the top to the freeway below and the WigWam on the other side.

B. Front gate to the WigWam

C. Side entrance to the WigWam, with buildings visible

A.   List of houses in the woods; Martin's name has been blacked out.

B.   The lane through the woods to the Martin's secluded home.

C.   Gary, curious about this road, discovered
Martin's house beyond the woods.

A. The two houses scouted but discarded as too populated.
This is on Route 310, just north of Route 40 in Etna, Ohio

B. A scouted but discarded house on Route
16 at the east side of Pataskala, Ohio

A. Annick's apartment.

B. View of garages across the street, where Annick was killed.

Map of Murder Sites

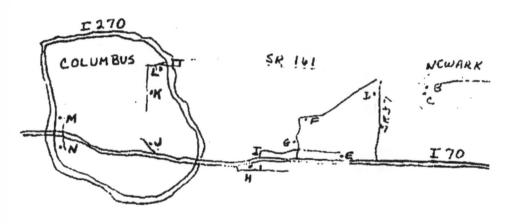

Legend:

A. Charles's farmhouse
B. Gary's Pine St. house
C. Forker's Cafe
D. Jenkin Jones's house
E. Gary's Kirkersville house
F. Pataskala house that was scouted
G. Etna house that was scouted
H. WigWam
I. Taylor Turnarounds
J. Annick's house
K. Gary's work—Rockwell Manufacturing
L. Martin's house
M. McCann's house
N. El Dorado Club

About the Author

JO ANN WIBLIN LIVES in Newark, Ohio, and is a retired grand-mother of three. She graduated from Ohio State University as a writing, literature, and physical education teacher in high school and college. She received her first Master's in Liberal Arts from Ohio University, and wrote a thesis entitled *Brothers in Murder*, which is soon to be a book. Later, she received a second Master's degree in Public Policy at the Ohio State University. She worked at the Mental Health Association of Licking County and wrote a column on local services. Later, she went to the Mental Health Association of Franklin County in Columbus, Ohio, as Executive Director. In these management roles, she spoke with mentally ill people, took battered women to shelters, led a family-support group, and worked on legislative issues in mental health.

After retirement, she wrote a humorous weekly gardening column for over three years, which is in the process of becoming a book entitled *Gardening: A Growing Addiction*.

Jo Ann is a devout Christian. She and her husband are active in their church.

She is very grateful to her husband, her professors, fellow students, the families of mentally ill, elderly people with great wisdom and history, and the public who received her writings well over the years.

CPSIA information can be obtained
at www.ICGtesting.com
Printed in the USA
BVHW081927280623
666449BV00006B/262

9 781638 744054